DESIGN AND ENGINEERING

CARS

Ian Graham

Raintree is an imprint of Capstone Global Library Limited, a company incorporated in England and Wales having its registered office at 7 Pilgrim Street, London, EC4V 6LB – Registered company number: 6695582

To contact Raintree please phone 0845 6044371, fax + 44 (0)1865 312263, or email myorders@raintreepublishers.co.uk. Customers from outside the UK please telephone +44 1865 312262.

Text © Capstone Global Library Limited 2013
First published in hardback in 2013
The moral rights of the proprietor have been asserted.

Edited by Andrew Farrow, Abby Colich, and
  Vaarunika Dharmapala
Designed by Richard Parker
Original illustrations © Capstone Global Library
  Ltd 2013
Illustrations by HL Studios
Picture research by Elizabeth Alexander
Originated by Capstone Global Library Ltd
Printed and bound in China by CTPS

ISBN 978 1 406 24974 3
16 15 14 13 12
10 9 8 7 6 5 4 3 2 1

British Library Cataloguing in Publication Data
Graham, Ian.
Cars. -- (Design and engineering)
629.2'22-dc23
A full catalogue record for this book is available from the British Library.

Acknowledgements
We would like to thank the following for permission to reproduce photographs: Alamy pp. 5 (© Dutourdumonde), 11 (© Transtock Inc.), 13 (© David Hoffman), 16 (© Jan Potente), 18 (© Jeremy Sutton-Hibbert), 23 (© CTK), 24 (© Cultura Creative), 29 & 43 (© Caro), 34 (© Jim West), 35 (© Bart Nedobre), 36 (© Richard Warburton); Corbis pp. 19 (© Transtock), 28 (© Matthias Hiekel/EPA), 45 (© C. Voigt); Getty Images pp. 7 (David Goddard), 12 (Slim Aarons), 22 (Bill Pugliano), 31 (Markel Redondo/Bloomberg via Getty Images), 32 (Johannes Simon), 37 (Tomohiro Ohsumi/Bloomberg via Getty Images), 38 (STR/AFP), 39 (Massimo Bettiol); © Google, Inc. p. 25; Shutterstock pp. 4 (© Adisa), 10 (© Vilius Steponenas), 14 top (© CHEN WS), 14 bottom (© Max Earey), 21 (© Gregor Kervina), 21 (© Alex Staroseltsev), 21, 33, 41 & 47 (© Michael Shake), 30 (© Geanina Bechea), 41 (© Alex Mit), 42 (© Andresr), 44 (© Devi), 47 (© Huguette Roe); design feature arrows Shutterstock (© MisterElements).

Cover photograph of a 2009 Lamborghini Gallardo LP 560-4 on a rural mountain racetrack reproduced with permission of Corbis (© Road and Track/Transtock).

Every effort has been made to contact copyright holders of material reproduced in this book. Any omissions will be rectified in subsequent printings if notice is given to the publisher.

CONTENTS

Some words are shown in bold, **like this**. You can find out what they mean by looking in the glossary.

DESIGNING AND MAKING CARS

Car manufacturing is one of the most important industries in the world. It is worth more than US$2 trillion a year. About 50 million people worldwide are employed in both car manufacturing and the thousands of businesses that depend on it.

An amazing product

Cars have made a dramatic impact on the quality of our lives. They have caused a revolution in personal mobility and transport for millions of people. They have also prompted great changes to our surroundings and the wider environment, as cobbled city streets and narrow country tracks were replaced by "metalled" (paved) roads more suitable for cars. However, as with many technologies, cars have significant disadvantages. For example, they have led to serious air pollution and congestion.

Every product has a **life cycle** – the time from its creation, sale, and use to its disposal at the end of its useful life. A small plastic toy might have a life cycle lasting only a few months. A car is built to last longer. A car's life cycle might be 15 years or more.

Each lane of a busy highway can carry up to about 2,000 cars per hour.

BUILDING A SUPERCAR

The McLaren MP4-12C is a 320-kilometres (200-miles) per hour supercar built by the same team that makes McLaren Formula 1 racing cars. It is made from tens of thousands of parts and every one of them had to be designed and manufactured. Engineers chose the size and shape of each part, decided which material it should be made from, and worked out how to manufacture it.

All cars go through a similar design and manufacturing process to the McLaren MP4-12C supercar.

Advancing technology

Buyers can choose from many different cars, so manufacturers work hard to make their products more attractive than those made by their rivals. The appearance of a car is just one aspect of its appeal. The technology built into it is important, too. Technology constantly advances through innovation and invention, which in turn is often driven by legislation (laws on safety, energy efficiency, and pollution). Engineers also adapt technology from other industries such as aerospace and defence, and also from motor racing. For instance, night vision technology was first developed for military use, but is now fitted to some cars to give drivers a clearer view in the dark.

WHAT IS TECHNOLOGY?

Technology is the process and result of using technical knowledge to modify natural materials for meeting human needs and wants. Companies will only invest time and money in researching materials, employing designers and engineers, and setting up car factories if they are confident there is demand for a car and that it will make them money.

Important terms

Throughout this book, you will come across some terms relating to the design and manufacturing of cars that also apply to other products. It might be helpful to explain some of these before you meet them so you can get more out of this book.

Requirements

There are two sorts of requirements:

- *Criteria*: goals that must be satisfied to make a successful product, for example, efficiency and appearance.
- *Constraints*: requirements limiting how the product is made, for example, cost and safety.

Balancing criteria and constraints is sometimes called a trade-off.

Engineering design

Engineering is the process of turning designs into real products. There is rarely a single, correct design solution to a problem. One solution is chosen from several options that are available.

Computer-Aided Engineering (CAE)

Car designers use computers in a process called **Computer-Aided Design (CAD)**. Using design information from CAD systems to control the machines and tools that make things is called **Computer-Aided Manufacturing (CAM)**. The whole process, from design to manufacturing, is also known as CAD/CAM. The use of techniques including CAD/CAM is called **Computer-Aided Engineering** (CAE).

Optimization

This is the process of improving a design to get the best possible product. Part of the optimization process is called **simulation**, which is the creation of realistic images or models to show how a new car might look in the real world. Optimization will include:

- *Modelling*: visualizing designs by using computer-generated images or clay models.
- *Prototyping*: making full-scale working models of designs.

Mass-produced cars are designed using Computer-Aided Design (CAD) systems, then manufactured in large numbers and shipped all over the world.

Component

Cars are made of lots of smaller parts, and these parts are called **components**. Car components can be simple parts such as nuts and bolts or bigger parts such as pumps or electric motors, which are themselves made of smaller components.

System

A group of pieces of machinery or processes that work together are called a **system**. For example, a car's steering wheel and the parts that connect it to the front wheels form the car's steering system.

Control

Control is the regulation or adjustment of a machine or process. Control can be applied manually or automatically. An example of manual control is the volume button on a television. Automatic systems are often controlled by computer chips called microprocessors. A typical car may have 50–100 microprocessors controlling its systems.

A CAR'S LIFE CYCLE

The life cycle of a car begins with a concept and ends with the destruction and disposal of the car at the end of its useful life.

The process of manufacturing begins with sourcing **raw materials**, for example in mines where rock containing metal is blasted out of the ground. About 65 per cent of an average car is made of iron and steel. The rest is made of other metals, plastic, rubber, and glass. Plastic is usually made from oil, although some is now made from plant material. Rubber for tyres is made from the milky sap of the rubber tree. Glass for the windows is made from silica sand. These raw materials are used to make the parts that are assembled in factories to produce cars.

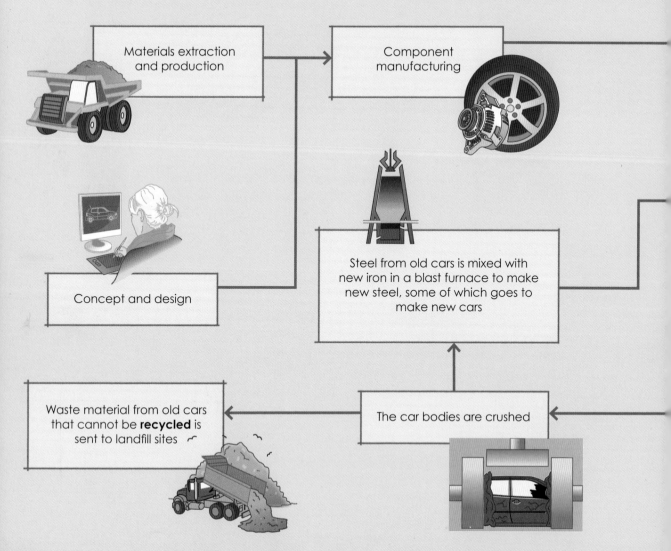

Materials extraction and production

Component manufacturing

Concept and design

Steel from old cars is mixed with new iron in a blast furnace to make new steel, some of which goes to make new cars

Waste material from old cars that cannot be **recycled** is sent to landfill sites

The car bodies are crushed

CONTRAST THE PAST

Modern cars last longer than early cars because of improved design, materials, and construction methods. Early cars were less reliable, too, and often broke down. A typical car in the 1920s lasted for six years. An average car today lasts for about 12 years. With careful maintenance it could easily last 20 years.

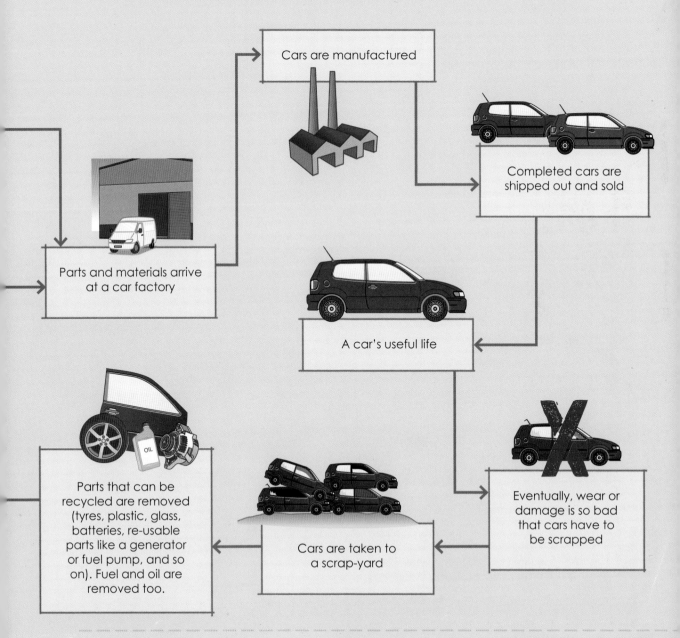

Cars are manufactured

Completed cars are shipped out and sold

Parts and materials arrive at a car factory

A car's useful life

Parts that can be recycled are removed (tyres, plastic, glass, batteries, re-usable parts like a generator or fuel pump, and so on). Fuel and oil are removed too.

Cars are taken to a scrap-yard

Eventually, wear or damage is so bad that cars have to be scrapped

MAKING PLANS

Developing a new car is extremely costly. The biggest manufacturers can spend US$500 million, or even more, before a single car is sold. Careful planning is essential for such an expensive project.

Planning

Planning for a new car usually begins three or four years before manufacturing starts. First, the manufacturer has to decide what type of car to build – sports cars, saloons, Sport Utility Vehicles (SUVs), hatchbacks, estates, supercars, kit cars, or luxury cars. Each type of car has a different set of features, capabilities, and performance that appeal to different motorists. Someone who wants a small sporty car to drive for fun will buy a different type of car from someone who wants to drive long distances in comfort, or someone who needs to transport a large family.

This is the BMW Vision Connected Drive concept car. Concept cars are built to test new ideas in car design (see page 11).

Market research

In order to produce successful cars, manufacturers need to know what motorists want. They gather this information by using market research. They ask people questions about the cars they already have and what sort of cars they might buy in the future. They also produce mock-ups (full-size models) called concept cars, to see what people think of them. They look at the products of rival manufacturers and take note of which models are the most successful.

Manufacturers also look out for trends in wider society. For example, when motorists started buying GPS satellite navigation units, manufacturers built satellite navigation into some of their cars. From all this research, they try to predict what people will want several years later when the new cars are due to go on sale.

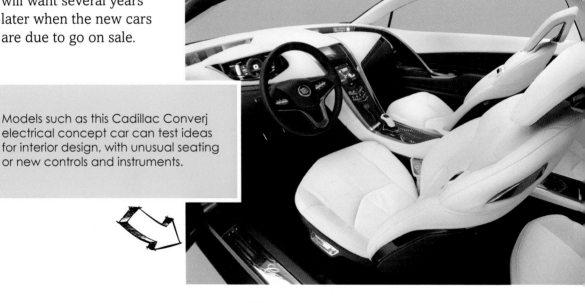

Models such as this Cadillac Converj electrical concept car can test ideas for interior design, with unusual seating or new controls and instruments.

MOTOR SHOWS

Motor shows are exhibitions where car-makers display the cars they are currently making and their ideas for future cars. The Frankfurt Motor Show is one of the world's oldest and biggest car shows. It started in 1897, when just eight cars were displayed. Some of the visitors then may never have seen a car before. At the 2011 show, 900 exhibitors from more than 30 countries displayed their cars and other auto products to nearly one million visitors.

Case study: the Nucleon nuclear-powered car

Car designers are always thinking about the next generation of cars. They sometimes try to look much further into the future, when some of the technical difficulties that make it impossible to build a certain type of car today have been solved. In the 1950s, Ford designers looked far into the future and imagined what a nuclear-powered car might be like.

Nuclear reactors need thick, heavy shielding to stop dangerous radiation from escaping. Ford's designers imagined a time when the shielding problem had been solved. The result was a car design called the Ford Nucleon. Its engine would work like a miniature nuclear submarine power plant. Uranium fuel in a nuclear "capsule" at the back of the car would heat water to make steam, which would drive two steam **turbines**, one to propel the car and the other to make electricity. Then the steam would be changed back into water and sent back through the reactor.

A nuclear-powered car like this would be able to go 8,000 kilometres (5,000 miles) before it had to be re-fuelled. A scale model of the car was made, but no **prototypes** were built, nor was the car ever manufactured. The shielding and radiation problems were never solved.

Here, William Ford, of the Ford company, stands by a model of the Nucleon. The concept behind this car never became reality.

Focus groups

Focus groups are used by manufacturers to find out about people's likes and dislikes. A small group of people, up to about a dozen, are invited to a meeting, where they are encouraged to talk about the product. It is not a question and answer session. The atmosphere is friendly and relaxed, and the group is given plenty of time to chat. In the case of cars, they might talk about anything from names to what made them buy a particular model, or what features they like. They might be shown some adverts and asked to discuss them. Microphones and cameras record everything for analysis later.

Focus groups are important to manufacturers. They provide insight into the way people think about and use products.

WHAT HAVE WE LEARNED?
- Planning for a new car begins three or four years before manufacturing.
- Planners have to predict what car buyers will want several years later.
- They carry out market research to find out what motorists want.
- They build concept cars to test new ideas.
- Finally, engineers begin designing the car that will actually be built.

DESIGNING NEW CARS

The design of a new car is a blend of science, engineering, art, fashion, and economics. Car designers have to balance these factors perfectly to produce a product that looks great, performs well, and can be manufactured.

What goes into a design?

A car is a collection of separate systems working together. These include lighting, steering, and braking systems. The engineers who design and develop cars have to include all of these in a new car.

One set of design criteria leads to a small, lightweight, nimble sports car. A different set leads to a big, rugged, heavy, and powerful SUV.

It is not possible to design a car that is the best at everything. A single car cannot be the fastest, most powerful, most fun to drive, most comfortable, most spacious, least expensive, most feature-laden, *and* most economical to run. Engineers have to decide which factors are priorities. This is called optimizing the design. Many of the design criteria – including size, weight, safety, and cost – have limits which the design must stay within. These limits are called **design constraints**.

Thinking about the life cycle

Engineers have to bear in mind the whole of a car's life cycle when they are creating new models. For example, they have to think about how it is going to be serviced and repaired. Mechanics need enough room inside, underneath, and in the engine bay to get at all the parts they might have to repair or replace. This affects the car's design.

Balancing science and fashion

Scientists can produce the most efficient shape for a car, one that slips through the air very easily. However, it may not be a shape people want to buy. So, a car's shape has as much to do with what is in fashion as it has to do with science and technology. A car buyer may decide whether he or she likes a car within 30 seconds of seeing it. Designers have to get its shape just right, or a potential sale could easily be lost.

CONTRAST THE PAST

The first cars were box-like in shape. Their designers did not understand how a car's shape affected the air flowing around it. However, most of these early cars were so slow that their shape did not matter, anyway.

Racing car designers started using shape to make faster cars in the 1950s. This practice spread to the design of ordinary cars in the 1980s. In this case, though, manufacturers were not trying to create faster cars, but rather ones that used less fuel.

Pencil, paper, and computers

A team of 30 or so designers works on a new car. They are divided into three groups. One works on the car's exterior. The second works on the interior. The third works on the car's colour and trim. The trim is all the extra features that are added to a car, including bumpers, door handles, and windscreen wipers.

The design of a new car begins with a drawing. Designers will try out lots of different shapes by making hundreds of drawings. To begin with, these drawings are made on paper.

Promising designs are copied into a CAD terminal. This allows the designers to create a three-dimensional image of the new car. They can create realistic moving images of cars in real street scenes to show what the finished cars will look like. These computer simulations enable the designers to try out different designs quickly.

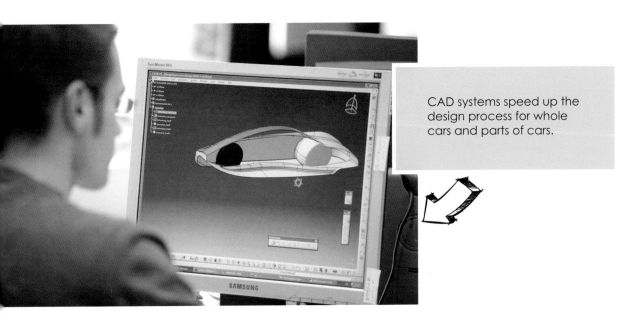

CAD systems speed up the design process for whole cars and parts of cars.

From design to cutting metal

Designing a car's shape is just one small part of the design process. The engine and other parts of the car are also designed, developed, and tested by engineers using computers. Designs for car parts on a CAD system are copied into a **Computer Aided Analysis (CAA)** system for testing. The strength and other properties of materials are programmed into the computer so it can determine how the parts are affected by forces, heat, and other factors. It can find weak points in a part where it might break or bend. Faults or weaknesses found at this stage can be put right before the part is made.

The information is then copied to a CAM system, which controls the machines that actually make the part. Designing, testing, and cutting all happen through CAE – remember, this stands for Computer-Aided Engineering. CAE saves time and minimizes costs because designers and engineers work with virtual parts and cars instead of having to build real parts and cars. A virtual object is one that exists as a mathematical model in a computer.

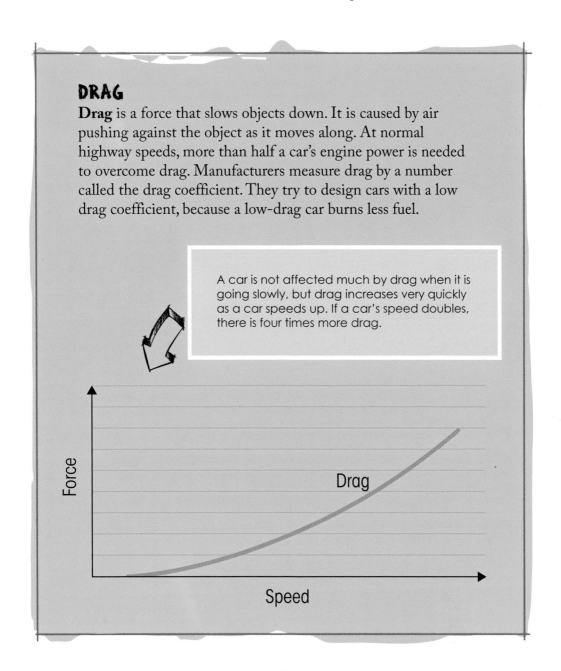

DRAG

Drag is a force that slows objects down. It is caused by air pushing against the object as it moves along. At normal highway speeds, more than half a car's engine power is needed to overcome drag. Manufacturers measure drag by a number called the drag coefficient. They try to design cars with a low drag coefficient, because a low-drag car burns less fuel.

A car is not affected much by drag when it is going slowly, but drag increases very quickly as a car speeds up. If a car's speed doubles, there is four times more drag.

Force

Drag

Speed

Modelling cars in clay

When engineers think they are close to the final design of a new car, they create models. The models are built from a metal and wood frame wrapped in foam plastic and covered with modelling clay. Clay is a traditional building and modelling material. It is used because it is inexpensive, easy to shape, simple to alter, and fast to work with.

A clay model shows what the real car will look like better than a picture on a flat screen or a sheet of paper. Models are made in all sizes, from small table-top ones to full-size ones. A full-size clay model, fitted with actual wheels, chrome trim, and gleaming paint, looks surprisingly realistic.

Clay models of new cars are built by professional model-makers.

Choosing materials

When designing a car, the engineers can choose which materials they use to make its parts. The materials are chosen for their properties and cost. Mass-produced cars have bodies made of steel, because it is easy to bend, cut, and drill. It is also readily available and less costly than other materials. More expensive cars sometimes have bodies made of aluminium, which is lighter than steel but pricier. The most expensive cars use carbon fibre, the lightest and most costly material of all.

Each material used in a car is chosen to suit the job it has to do:
- metal pipes and rubber hoses carry fluids between parts of the car
- plastic-coated wire connects electrical parts together
- plastic, textiles, and other soft materials are used in the interior
- tyres are made of rubber which has been strengthened with steel cords
- windows are made of glass.

CONTRAST THE PAST

The designers who create the shapes of new cars are influenced by all sorts of factors, including the most exciting technologies of the day. In the late 1950s and early 1960s, the Space Age had just begun. Rockets were the latest thing in advanced technology. Car designers in the United States (and later elsewhere in the world) produced cars with tailfins similar to the fins on rockets. They had no practical use, but the designers thought they would be popular. They were right!

Protecting designs

It costs a great deal of money to develop new cars and the parts they need. Manufacturers will, of course, want to prevent other car-makers from copying their unique designs. If manufacturers develop a new **device** or part, they can stop other people from copying it by means of a **patent**. A patent is an official record of what the invention is and who owns it. Anyone else who wants to make the same device, sell it, or use it in their products, must have the permission of the patent holder and, usually, pay for its use. Modern cars incorporate inventions covered by more than 100,000 patents.

Patents are used to protect inventions. Designs, names, words, images, and symbols are protected in another way. They can be registered as trademarks. A car manufacturer who creates a name or a symbol to represent a car, or part of a car, will register it as a trademark. In a similar way to patents, this then prevents anyone else from using the name or symbol without authorization from the owner.

VOICE COMMAND

Some car equipment can be controlled by the driver's voice instead of by using switches and buttons. A microphone picks up the driver's voice, which is then changed into computer code. This is done by a part called an analogue to digital converter. The stream of digital code is divided up into a series of short segments.

The system compares the pattern of the short segments with digital sounds called phonemes in its memory. Phonemes are the shortest sounds that make up speech, like the *a* in cat, or *ur* in burn. There are about 40 phonemes in English. The system analyses the string of phonemes to work out the words that have been spoken. It then carries out the required operation, which might be to turn up the radio volume or operate an integrated MP3 player. One advantage of voice command is that the driver does not need to take his or her hands off the steering wheel to carry out some operations.

THE NUMBER OF CARS IN THE WORLD

There are more than 600 million cars worldwide.

If all these cars were parked in a straight line, nose to tail, they would stretch around the equator 67.5 times.

If they were piled on top of each other, the heap would be 900,000 kilometres (559,000 miles) high.

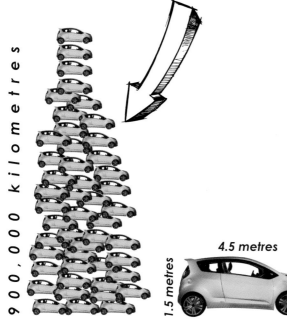

900,000 kilometres

4.5 metres

1.5 metres

The distance from Earth to the Moon is 384,400 kilometres (238,855 miles). All the cars in the world would cover that distance seven times over.

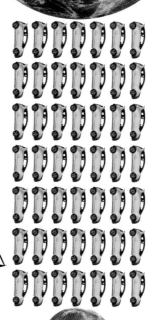

The maths:
A car measures about 4.5 metres (14.8 feet) long.
So, 600 million cars x 4.5 metres = 2.7 million kilometres (1.7 million miles) long. Earth's circumference is roughly 40,000 kilometres (25,000 miles).

A car measures about 1.5 metres (4.9 feet) high. So, 600 million cars x 1.5 metres = 900,000 kilometres (559,000 miles).

A line of cars 2.7 million kilometres (1.7 million miles) long ÷ the distance to the Moon, 384,400 kilometres (238,855 miles) = 7.02.

The model range

Several different versions of each car are built, from a basic model to a top-of-the-range one with lots of extra features. The various models are aimed at motorists with different needs. The choices they are offered include two-door or four-door, petrol or diesel engine, small engine or bigger engine, and different levels of fittings and features.

Testing new cars

All new cars are tested thoroughly. Many of these tests are performed by computers, using virtual cars. The next step is to build working prototypes for testing. Prototypes are the first examples of a product to be built, and are put through lots of different tests. There are crash tests, high-speed driving tests, tests on bumpy roads, vibration tests, tests in strong crosswinds, wet road driving tests, brake tests, low temperature tests, radio interference tests, wind tunnel tests, and driving tests in different regions of the world with different climates. The car's interior is also tested for comfort and practicality. The positions and ease of use of controls and instruments are checked.

In a wind tunnel test, air is blown through a tunnel to study the way it flows around the shape of the car.

Problems and faults are nearly always found in the prototypes. These are put right by a process called **troubleshooting**. The modified prototypes are tested again. Finally, the production model of the car can be manufactured in large numbers.

Crash test dummies

Prototype cars are deliberately crashed to find out how safe they are. The tests help them to meet international safety standards. Mechanical models of drivers and passengers, called crash test dummies, sit in the cars. The dummies are fitted with dozens of **sensors** that collect tens of thousands of readings during a crash that lasts for just a fraction of a second.

Dummies take the place of real people in car crash tests. The dummies have flexible joints and weigh the same as people.

CONTRAST THE PAST

The first tests to find out what happens to people in cars and planes during crashes were carried out in the 1930s in the United States. They used human cadavers (dead bodies). However, bodies were not ideal, because they were all different from each other, making it difficult to compare tests, and they were in short supply. Animals were also tried, but they were not the same as each other either, or the same as people. So, the crash test dummy was invented in 1949 to replace them. The first crash test dummy was called Sierra Sam.

New types of engines

Manufacturers are developing cars that are more energy-efficient throughout their whole life cycle. A key factor is the development of new types of engines that burn less fuel, or burn no fuel at all. **Hybrid cars** such as the Toyota Prius have a petrol engine and an electric motor. The electric motor powers the car some of the time, saving fuel.

Other cars require no fuel at all. They use electricity from batteries as their energy source. However, manufacturing and disposing of batteries, which contain heavy metals such as lead, can cause pollution. Furthermore, the electricity that recharges them may come from coal-fired power stations, which can also cause pollution. Another type of electric car is powered by a device called a **fuel cell**. This uses a chemical reaction between a fuel and oxygen in the air to produce electricity. Yet another new type of car engine burns hydrogen gas. Water vapour, instead of harmful pollutants, comes out of its exhaust pipe.

When a battery-powered car runs low on energy, it is plugged into an electricity supply to recharge its batteries.

Cars without drivers

Every year, more than a million people die and 50 million are injured in road accidents around the world. Nearly all car accidents are caused by human error. Researchers have found that computers can drive cars more safely than people – they do not get distracted or tired, and they are never in a hurry.

The first computer-controlled cars could drive themselves only on very simple test tracks. The latest robot cars are able to go on real roads. Self-driving cars developed by Google (below) have been driving on public roads at normal speeds in California, USA, for several years. They have covered more than 250,000 kilometres (155,000 miles). These cars use cameras, radar, and lasers to build up a picture of the road ahead and the nearby traffic. Computers control the engine and steer the car. The German manufacturer, Volkswagen, has also developed a car that can drive itself safely at motorway speeds in traffic.

WHAT HAVE WE LEARNED?
- Designs are the product of many inputs (factors) including fashion, safety, technology, materials, cost, and environmental concerns.
- Inputs change, and so designs will also change.
- Designs are optimized according to certain criteria or constraints, such as ruggedness (4x4s) or sporty performance (sports cars).
- Prototypes are built to test designs.
- Cars will be lighter and burn less fuel in the future.
- Driverless cars are already being tested in real traffic on public roads.

BUILDING A CAR FACTORY

Most new cars are built in existing factories, but sometimes a manufacturer will build a brand new facility to produce a car. It is a big, expensive project that needs careful planning.

Deciding the location

A suitable location for a factory should have good transport links and plenty of space to extend it in the future. It should also be in a peaceful country with low taxes, reliable power supplies, and lots of potential workers living nearby.

If the factory is built in a place with low wages, labour costs can be kept down. However, wages may be low because the local people have poor levels of education and skills. In this case, training costs may be high. One solution is to locate in a high-wage, well-educated region, but use automation, machines, and robots where possible to increase productivity and keep wage costs down.

ECONOMY OF SCALE

When a product is made in large numbers, the cost of each one falls. This is because the total cost of production is spread across a greater number of products. This is called the **economy of scale**.

RECORD BREAKER

The world's biggest car factory belongs to the Korean car-maker, Hyundai. Its factory in Ulsan, South Korea, employs 34,000 people and produces 1.5 million cars a year.

How big?

How big a factory should be depends on how many cars it will produce. Machines and robots are positioned so the cars can move smoothly through the factory from one construction stage to the next without delays. A large area outside the factory has to be set aside for parking the completed cars until they can be collected. A track for test-drives has to be fitted in, too.

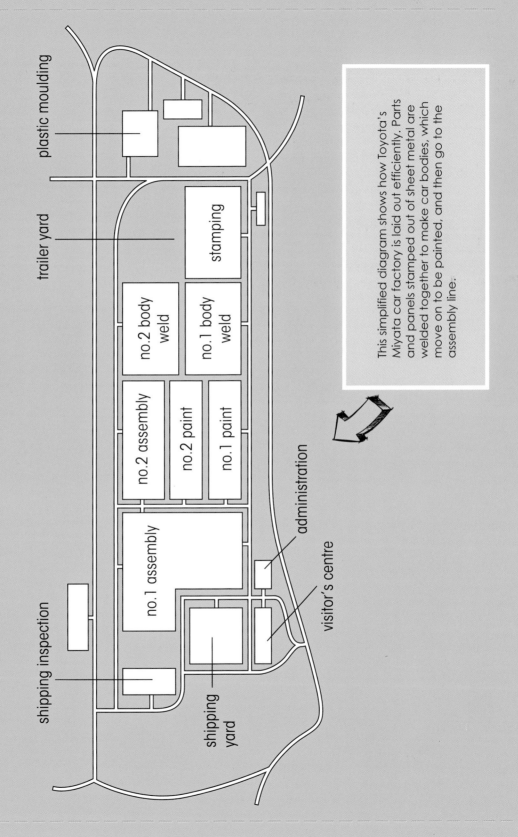

plastic moulding

trailer yard

shipping inspection

no.2 body weld

no.1 body weld

stamping

no.2 assembly

no.2 paint

no.1 paint

no.1 assembly

shipping yard

administration

visitor's centre

This simplified diagram shows how Toyota's Miyata car factory is laid out efficiently. Parts and panels stamped out of sheet metal are welded together to make car bodies, which move on to be painted, and then go to the assembly line.

Case study: the see-through factory

Volkswagen's Gläserne Manufaktur in Dresden, Germany, is a very unusual car factory. Its name means "factory made of glass" or "transparent factory". Most of its walls are made of glass. Inside, the assembly line is clean and quiet. The cars glide through the factory slowly and silently on moving floor panels.

Up to 250 people a day visit the factory and look through the glass walls to see the cars being built. Car buyers can then collect their new cars. Cars awaiting collection are stored in the Vehicle Tower, a 40-metre (130-feet) high glass tower, which can hold 280 cars on 16 floors.

Cars are carried from one floor to another by giant metal arms hanging from a rail in the ceiling.

The cars are thoroughly tested before they are handed over to buyers. First, they are given test drives on the factory's two 250-metre (820-feet) test tracks. These tracks have bumpy sections that shake the cars about. The drivers listen to the sounds the cars make as they vibrate over the bumps. They can pick out any unusual sounds that might signal a problem. Finally, the cars are test driven on a 10-kilometre (6-mile) track as well as on city streets and motorways to check everything is working correctly.

Looking after the environment

The Gläserne Manufaktur's designers were keen to make the factory environmentally friendly. Outside, the building is surrounded by trees, grass, and ponds. Loudspeakers play the sound of birdsong. The outside lighting is yellow, chosen so it does not disturb insects in a nearby botanical garden.

More air pollution and traffic congestion in Dresden is avoided by delivering some parts and materials to the factory by train instead of lorries. Volkswagen's own freight trains deliver 60 tonnes at a time, taking the place of three lorries on every journey.

A central hoist slots each completed car into its own parking spot in the glittering glass Vehicle Tower.

WHAT HAVE WE LEARNED?
- Car factories need lots of space to start with as well as space to grow.
- They must be close to roads and ports.
- The layout must be logical and efficient to avoid delays.
- Machines, automation, and robots increase productivity, cut costs, and improve quality.
- Car factories can be calm, clean, and as attractive as an art gallery.

MANUFACTURING CARS

More than 50 million cars are built every year. Manufacturing each and every one of them involves using tools and machines to change materials and to assemble parts.

A network of suppliers

Car manufacturing depends on a complicated worldwide network of industries, transport, communication, and factories. A car factory and its suppliers depend on each other. A shortage of materials or a delay in the supply of parts can bring a car factory to a standstill. A shutdown in car production can bring suppliers' factories to a standstill, too, because there is suddenly no demand for their products.

These rolls of steel will be used to build cars. Each roll weighs as much as 10 completed vehicles.

Manufacturing processes

The processes that transform steel and other materials into finished cars include **blanking**, **stamping**, forging, casting, welding, and **machining**. Steel arrives at a car factory in giant rolls. It is fed into blanking machines that flatten it and cut out smaller sheets. The sheets are loaded into stamping machines that press and bend them. They are then welded together to make a car's body. Welding involves heating spots or edges of two pieces of steel so they melt and join together.

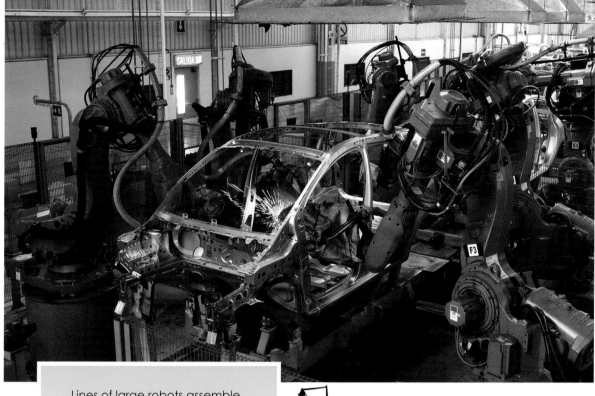

Lines of large robots assemble and weld the bodies of cars.

Some parts are made by a process called forging. In forging, a piece of metal is hammered to change its shape. The metal is placed on a mould called a die. Then a mechanical hammer is dropped on the metal, forcing it into the shape of the die. Car wheels are made by forging.

Casting is a process that involves pouring molten metal into a mould so the metal takes up the shape of the mould. Car engine blocks are made by casting. Parts made by forging or casting are finished off by machining them. This involves using **machine tools** to drill, cut, or shave metal from the casting until it reaches its final shape.

ROBOTS

Most of the welding and painting work in a car factory is done by robots. A large factory may have several hundred of them. Unlike human workers, robots can work non-stop and produce high quality work 24 hours a day if necessary. The robots have to be programmed to do their jobs. Ryo Shimizu, a robot programmer for Toyota, says, "I carefully analyse the movements of experienced workers and program the robots so they make the same movements."

Case study: painting a car body

Thousands of small processes combine to make a car. Let's look at just one part of making a car – painting the body – to see how detailed these processes can be.

Car bodies are painted in a series of controlled stages. The bare metal body is cleaned and painted with several coats of paint. This work is carried out in a clean, dust-free environment. The numbers of cars painted in each colour are chosen according to the numbers of orders for each colour received by dealers.

The body is washed several times in a chemical bath to remove any dirt, oil, or grease that might prevent the first coat of paint sticking. This is sometimes called pretreatment. Then the whole car body is lowered into a tank of liquid primer, or e-coat. The glossy paint that gives the car its colour does not stick to bare metal very well, so the primer's job is to provide a better surface for the next coat of paint. An electric current passes through the primer and car body, drawing the primer into every part of the body. It is vital to cover all the metal so that rain and moisture cannot reach it later and make it rust.

Robot arms are spraying a fine mist of paint on to a car body. The arms are programmed to coat the whole body evenly.

Next, workers or robots spray a coat of paint called surfacer, or intermediate coat, on the body. This helps to smooth the surface, ready for the next coat of paint, the topcoat. The topcoat, sprayed on by workers or robots, gives the car its final colour. A clear varnish, or clearcoat, may be sprayed on top of this to give the paint a mirror-like surface or metallic sheen.

Drying and curing

Between coats of paint, the car body is baked in an oven at 100–180°C (212–356°F). This not only dries the paint, but also cures it. Curing is a chemical process. The paint contains chain-like chemicals called polymers. Inside the oven, heat makes these polymer chains lock together, hardening the paint. The finished paint job is inspected in minute detail under bright lighting to ensure that there are no defects. The whole painting process takes about nine hours for each car.

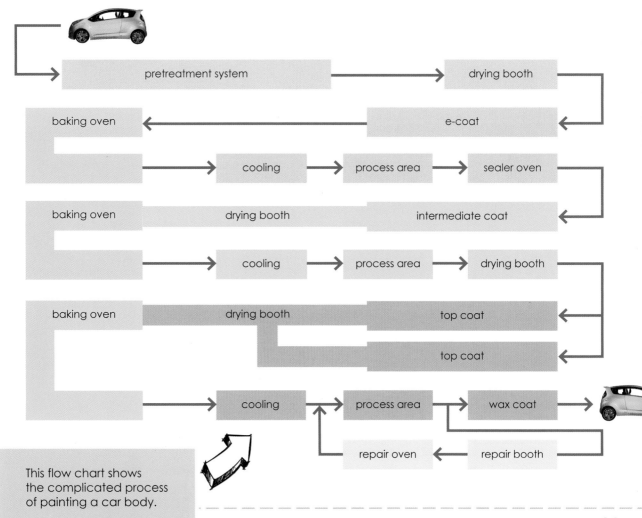

This flow chart shows the complicated process of painting a car body.

The assembly line

After painting, the body moves on to the assembly line. Here, car bodies move along while workers fit parts on to them. The bodies are fitted with wiring, electronic components, and the dashboard. Meanwhile, the running gear has been built. The running gear includes the steering, **suspension**, engine, and gearbox. The body is lowered on to the running gear and the two are bolted together. The interior of the car is fitted with seats, carpets, and roof lining. The wheels are fitted and fuel, oil, and water are added. Then the car is started for the first time. The engine's performance is checked and the whole car is inspected to make sure that everything looks and works as it should.

An assembly line is an efficient way to produce large numbers of cars quickly.

Sourcing parts

A typical car is built from about 30,000 parts, or components. They come from suppliers all over the world. Car-makers aim to buy only as many parts as they need and to have them delivered just before they are used. This is known as "just in time". Its advantages include reducing the car-maker's costs and the amount of space needed to store parts. However, it has disadvantages, too. Any interruption in the supply of parts quickly brings car production to a halt.

Engine manufacturing

Engine manufacturing begins by pouring molten iron into a mould to make the engine block. The rough casting is then drilled and machined to make it the correct shape, with bolt-holes for attaching other parts. A typical engine is made from more than 500 parts.

Factories that make parts for cars have their own assembly lines where the parts are made and inspected before being dispatched to car-makers.

CONTRAST THE PAST

The car assembly line was invented in 1901 by Ransom Eli Olds, who founded the American Oldsmobile car company. In 1913, another American car-maker, Henry Ford, introduced the moving assembly line. Cars on a moving assembly line move along while they are being built. Ford got the idea from slaughterhouses, where farm animals were butchered as they moved along a conveyor. Ford's most famous car in the early 1900s was the Model T. The moving assembly line enabled Ford to build a Model T in 93 minutes compared to the more than 12 hours it took by traditional methods.

Controlling quality

Making sure that every car is as good as it can be is called **quality control**. The parts a car is built from and the whole car itself are checked at every stage to make sure they are precisely the right size and shape, and have been fitted in exactly the right position. Robots often do this checking work because they can do it quickly with great precision.

Some inspection systems use lasers to measure the positions of parts to within a tenth of a millimetre – about the width of a human hair! Positioning a car's doors and body panels this accurately helps make the car quieter inside, cutting the noise caused by air flowing around the body. In 2011, Ford spent US$100 million on robotic laser inspection equipment for 17 of its factories.

HAND BUILT CARS

Not all cars are mass-produced on moving assembly lines in vast factories. Some are made by hand in small numbers. The cars stay in one place and workers bring the parts to them. Some manufacturers use the fact that their cars are built in small numbers by craftsmen as a selling point. Racing cars, such as the Aston Martin above, are hand-built in this way, too.

The vast decks of car transport ships are like floating car parks. This ship is about to load up with completed cars.

Delivering cars

If a new car passes all its inspections and tests, it is finally allowed to join the rest that are parked outside awaiting collection. So many cars have to be transported from factories to dealers in different countries that transporter lorries and ships have been built specially for the job. A large car transporter ship can carry up to 6,000 cars.

A mass-produced car is usually delivered about four weeks after it is ordered. Specialist or "marque" cars that are built in small numbers sometimes have long waiting lists of buyers. They may have to wait up to two years for their cars to be built and delivered. The cars are so desirable that customers are prepared to wait.

WHAT HAVE WE LEARNED?
- Car factories take in parts and materials, and transform them into finished cars.
- Mass-produced cars are built on moving assembly lines.
- Robots and other machines do a lot of the work in car factories.

MARKETING

Marketing is a vital part of the car industry. Every new car is accompanied by a marketing campaign. This involves informing people about the car and its various features, and showing how the car meets the customers' needs.

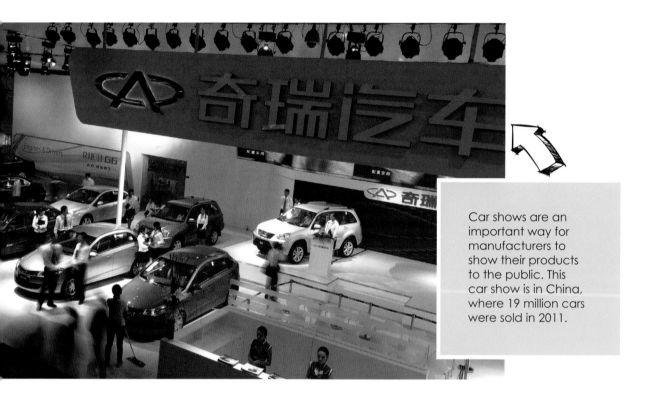

Car shows are an important way for manufacturers to show their products to the public. This car show is in China, where 19 million cars were sold in 2011.

Appealing to the customer

Manufacturers try to make their cars more attractive by linking them with positive qualities such as comfort, luxury, reliability, glamour, fun, or environmental friendliness. The name of a car is chosen to match the qualities it is linked to. Sports cars often have names linked with power. The Ford Mustang is named after a World War II fighter plane and a wild horse. SUVs may have names linked to their off-road abilities, such as the Ford Explorer and the Toyota Land Cruiser. Names linked to places, history, mythology, and nature are popular, too.

Car-makers have to be careful with their choice of names. A name that seems to be a perfect choice in one language may mean something different or rude in another language! Some manufacturers prefer to give their cars model numbers instead of names, or they will make up names. The Renault Twingo, for example, is a combination of the words twist, swing, and tango.

ADVERTISING

Press, radio, and television advertisements reinforce a car's image and show buyers how a car can fit in with their lifestyle or improve their quality of life. Particular models are marketed to specific buyers. An advert for a family car might show it comfortably fitting in a whole family and all their shopping or holiday luggage. An advert for a sports car might show an open-top being driven on a long, winding, empty road through a wilderness by a driver who is clearly enjoying the experience.

Manufacturers can get valuable publicity if their cars win rallies and races.

WHAT HAVE WE LEARNED?

- Manufacturers create an attractive image or story to accompany a car.
- Advertising repeats this image or story over and over again.
- Winning motor races can make certain cars more popular with buyers.

THE LIFE OF A CAR

A manufacturer's link with a new car does not stop when it is sold. They continue to provide support and training for dealers and mechanics who service and repair the cars.

Keeping cars in working order

A car is a complex machine with lots of moving parts that gradually wear out. To keep a car in good working order, it has to be checked every year or so and have worn-out parts replaced. These regular check-ups are called services. A car can be serviced in any suitably equipped garage, but the dealers that sell a particular manufacturer's cars have all the specialist knowledge, training, and tools needed to do the job to the manufacturer's specifications. The mechanics who work for car dealers go on training courses run by manufacturers to learn exactly how to service and repair their cars.

In a typical service, dozens of items are checked and, if necessary, adjusted or replaced.

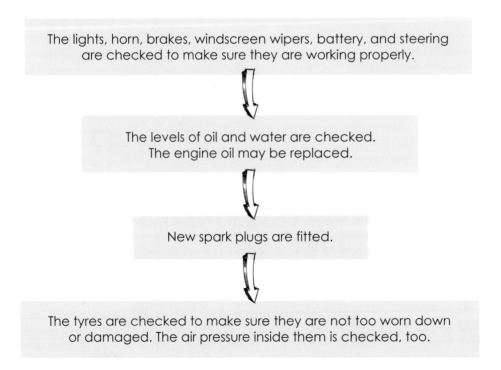

The lights, horn, brakes, windscreen wipers, battery, and steering are checked to make sure they are working properly.

The levels of oil and water are checked. The engine oil may be replaced.

New spark plugs are fitted.

The tyres are checked to make sure they are not too worn down or damaged. The air pressure inside them is checked, too.

As a car gets older, it needs more work to keep it in good condition. More parts wear out and have to be replaced. Eventually, its first owner sells it. A car may be bought and sold several times.

IN A LIFETIME

The average US driver gets through **31,350 US GALLONS OF FUEL** during a lifetime of driving the equivalent of 25 times around the world (more than 1 million kilometres or 627,000 miles) in five different cars.

US DRIVER'S LIFETIME

31,350 US GALLONS

+

+

=

+

+

+

31,350 US gallons is equivalent to almost **THREE AND A HALF OF THE BIGGEST ROAD TANKER TRUCKS** holding 9,000 US gallons each.

Repairs

When a car develops a fault or breaks down, it has to be repaired. Car owners with some mechanical knowledge and ability can carry out some simple repairs themselves. However, as cars have become more advanced, more and more of the repair and maintenance work has to be done in garages by professionally trained mechanics.

Garages often have lifts that can raise a car off the ground so a mechanic can work on it from underneath.

Downloading data

Many cars have a built-in computer that mechanics can connect to a terminal in the garage, called a diagnostic computer. This can download all sorts of information about the car's systems and how they have been working. The car's computer keeps a record of any problems that have occurred and this helps a mechanic to trace faults.

Safety first

In many countries, cars must have regular tests to make sure they are safe and are not producing too much air pollution. The mechanical condition of the cars is checked to make sure nothing is broken, loose, or dangerous. The depth of the tread on the tyres is checked and the headlights are tested to make sure they point in the right direction.

Occasionally, after cars have been sold, a manufacturer discovers that a part is faulty or has been fitted wrongly. If the problem affects the car's safety, the manufacturer may issue a recall notice, which tells owners to bring their cars to a dealer to have the problem put right.

This mechanic is testing a car using a diagnostic computer. The results of the test appear on the computer's screen.

THE ENGINE CONTROL UNIT

Most cars have a computer called the engine control unit (ECU). Its job is to keep the engine running as efficiently as possible. This saves fuel and reduces harmful **exhaust emissions**. Dozens of sensors on the engine and driving controls collect information and send it to the ECU. The ECU then calculates how much fuel and air to send to the engine, when to open and close the valves that let them in, and when to fire the sparks that ignite the fuel in some engines.

The environmental impact of cars

Cars affect the environment in many ways. Their engines give out gases that become part of the air we breathe. Vast areas of countryside have been covered with concrete and asphalt to make roads and car parks. The vast majority of cars have engines that burn a fuel made from oil. Oil spilled from oil wells and from tanker ships wrecked at sea damages marine life and coasts.

Burning fuel in a car engine produces particles and gases called exhaust emissions. An average car's exhaust emissions contain more than 1,000 different chemicals. Many of them are harmful to people and the environment. Some are harmful because they can cause breathing problems. Others combine with moisture in the air and form acid rain, which can kill plants.

Some exhaust emissions are greenhouse gases. They trap energy from the Sun and warm Earth's atmosphere. Most climate scientists think the atmosphere is warming enough to change the climate. This is called global warming. Noise pollution near busy roads can be a big problem, too.

Cars depend on a worldwide network of fuel stations. Oil from oil wells is shipped to refineries, which produce fuel. Ships and trucks then deliver it to fuel stations.

Cleaner cars

Most car engines are now fitted with a device called a **catalytic converter**, which reduces the amount of harmful gases given out. Gases from the engine pass through a honeycomb coated with rare metals including platinum, rhodium, and palladium. They cause chemical reactions in the gases that change harmful substances such as unburned fuel, carbon monoxide, and nitrogen oxide into less harmful gases such as carbon dioxide and nitrogen.

Catalytic converters cannot deal with all the gases that pass through them, so engine exhaust emissions still cause problems. In big cities in sunny, warm, dry parts of the world, sunlight acting on exhaust emissions causes chemical reactions that can produce a harmful foggy cloud called photochemical smog.

Sports stadiums, shopping centres, and other large buildings require thousands of parking spaces for all the people who will work in them and visit them.

WHAT HAVE WE LEARNED?
- Cars require regular servicing to keep them in good working condition.
- Parts sometimes break or wear out and have to be replaced.
- A car may be bought and sold several times during its useful life.
- Burning fuel in a car engine produces chemicals that pollute the air.
- Catalytic converters can make car engines less polluting.

DISPOSAL AND RECYCLING

When a car is so old or in such poor condition that no-one wants it, it has to be disposed of. A surprising amount of material and parts can be removed from these "scrappers" and used again.

Scrapping

At the end of their useful life, cars are sent to dismantlers and scrapyards for disposal. In Europe, 8–9 million cars are scrapped every year. More than three-quarters of the parts and materials these cars are made from are recovered and recycled instead of sending them to a waste dump. Reuse and recycling reduces the **environmental impact** of cars. It stops old wrecked cars from piling up, rusting away, and leaking fuel and oil into the ground. It also saves money, energy, and raw materials.

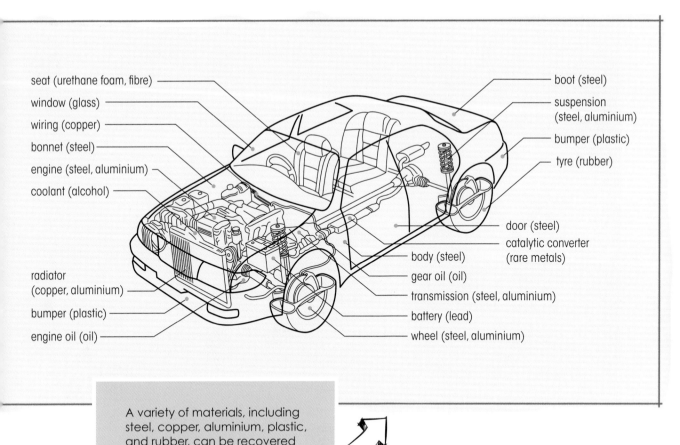

seat (urethane foam, fibre)
window (glass)
wiring (copper)
bonnet (steel)
engine (steel, aluminium)
coolant (alcohol)
radiator (copper, aluminium)
bumper (plastic)
engine oil (oil)

boot (steel)
suspension (steel, aluminium)
bumper (plastic)
tyre (rubber)
door (steel)
catalytic converter (rare metals)
body (steel)
gear oil (oil)
transmission (steel, aluminium)
battery (lead)
wheel (steel, aluminium)

A variety of materials, including steel, copper, aluminium, plastic, and rubber, can be recovered from cars at the end of their useful life and re-used.

Car bodies arrive at a scrapyard and are piled up until they can be crushed. The crusher reduces each car to a block of metal the size of a fridge.

STEEL

ALUMINIUM

THE AVERAGE CAR CONTAINS:

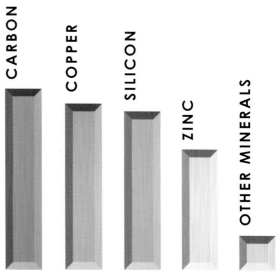

- more than a tonne of steel
- 108 kilograms (240 pounds) of aluminium
- 23 kilograms (50 pounds) of carbon
- 19 kilograms (42 pounds) of copper
- 18 kilograms (41 pounds) of silicon
- 10 kilograms (22 pounds) of zinc
- more than 30 other minerals including titanium, platinum, and gold.

CARBON

COPPER

SILICON

ZINC

OTHER MINERALS

Crushing and shredding

When all the useful parts, oil, fuel, and other materials have been removed from a scrapped car, the body is crushed to a standard size to make it easier to transport to a processing plant. There, it is shredded into tiny pieces so the different metals can be separated more easily. The leftover mixture of plastic, rubber, and metal is called automobile shredder residue (ASR). This used to be buried in the ground at landfill sites, but now car manufacturers take it back and recover even more materials from it.

Some of the materials recovered from old cars are used to make new ones. Hybrid, electric, and hydrogen-powered cars will one day be made from materials yet to be recovered from cars that are still being driven today.

Recovered materials

Steel and other metals from old cars may be used to make a wide range of metal products.

Aluminium from scrapped cars could end up being used to make drinks cans.

The rare metals in catalytic converters are recovered and used to make new catalytic converters.

Engine oil can be recycled as fuel for boilers and incinerators.

Foam plastic and fibre from car seats are used to make soundproofing materials.

Lead from car batteries is used to make new batteries.

WHAT HAPPENS TO RUBBER?

A car contains about 50 kilograms (110 pounds) of rubber, mainly in its tyres. Some tyres are in such good condition that they can be re-sold and used by other cars. Worn-down tyres can be re-moulded to make new tyres. Tyres that are too badly damaged for re-moulding are ground up into tiny crumbs and used to make flooring, sports pitches, playground surfaces, and roads. The rest are burned.

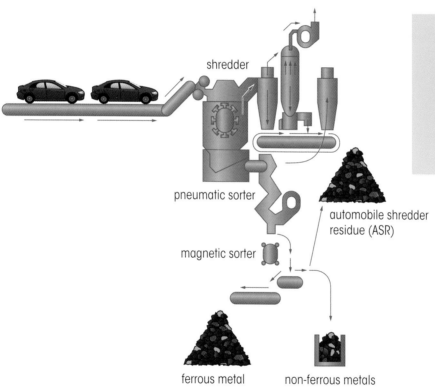

shredder

pneumatic sorter

automobile shredder residue (ASR)

magnetic sorter

ferrous metal

non-ferrous metals

When a scrapped car is shredded into tiny bits, a magnet separates the ferrous metals (iron and steel) from the non-ferrous metals such as copper and aluminium.

WHAT HAVE WE LEARNED?
- Tens of millions of cars are scrapped every year.
- Their parts and materials are recycled and used to make new cars.
- Magnets separate ferrous metals from other materials, because ferrous metals stick to magnets.

TIMELINE

1478   The Italian artist, scientist, and engineer Leonardo da Vinci designs the first self-propelled car. It was to be powered by the energy stored in wound-up springs. However, Leonardo never actually built his car.

1672   A priest called Ferdinand Verbiest builds the first working automobile (self-propelled vehicle). It is a small model steam-powered car built as a toy for the emperor of China.

1769   French inventor Nicolas-Joseph Cugnot builds the first full-size working self-propelled vehicle. It is an ungainly three-wheeled steam-powered tractor.

1885   German engineer Karl Benz builds the world's first motor car – a car powered by an internal combustion engine instead of a steam engine.

1901   American Ransom Eli Olds invents the assembly line method for building cars. It enables his factory to produce more than five times as many cars as before.

1913   Henry Ford builds the first moving car assembly line to build Model T cars. It enables him to become the world's biggest car manufacturer.

1921   German inventor Edmund Rumpler designs the Rumpler-Tropfenauto (tear-drop car) with a shape based on a teardrop, the most aerodynamic shape in nature.

1934   The US car manufacturer Chrysler produces a car called the Airflow, with a shape inspired by birds and aircraft in flight. It is one of the first cars to be designed with the help of wind tunnel tests.

1949   The first crash test dummy, called Sierra Sam, is created to test aircraft ejection seats. Later, in the 1950s, crash test dummies are used to test cars.

1953   The Chevrolet Corvette sports car appears as a concept car at a motor show called the GM Motorama in New York City, USA. It is so popular that the US car manufacturer General Motors decide to manufacture it immediately. The Corvette is in production only six months later and has continued in production until the present day.

1957 Ford produces a design for a nuclear-powered car of the future called the Nucleon. It is never manufactured.

1961 The first industrial robot, called Unimate, is installed in a General Motors car factory in New Jersey, USA, to stack hot metal castings.

1964 IBM develops the forerunner of modern Computer-Aided Design (CAD). Their computer software, called DAC-1 (Design Augmented by Computer), is used by designers at General Motors to help design cars.

1973 A worldwide energy crisis causes a steep rise in oil prices, forcing car and engine designers to think more carefully about how much fuel their cars use.

1978 The first anti-lock braking system (ABS) is developed by Bosch in Germany. It helps cars to stop more quickly without skidding.

1997 A jet-propelled car called Thrust SSC with a shape designed by British aerodynamicist Ron Ayers becomes the first car to set a land speed record faster than the speed of sound. On 15 October 1997, it sets a supersonic land speed record of 1,228 kilometres (763 miles) per hour.

2002 Volkswagen opens its Gläserne Manufaktur (see-through factory) for building cars in the German city of Dresden.

GLOSSARY

blanking cutting pieces out of a continuous strip of material, called a web. In car manufacturing, the web is a roll of sheet steel and the shapes cut out of it are used for making parts of car bodies.

catalytic converter part of a car that changes harmful exhaust gases from the car's engine into less harmful gases by means of chemical reactions

component part of something bigger

Computer-Aided Analysis (CAA) use of computers to analyse or test designs

Computer-Aided Design (CAD) use of computer technology for the process of designing objects

Computer-Aided Engineering (CAE) use of computerised design, testing, and manufacturing techniques such as CAD/CAM and CAA

Computer-Aided Manufacturing (CAM) use of information and computer technology in the manufacture of products, normally in conjunction with CAD

design constraints limitations on how something is made

device machine, part, or tool that carries out a specific task

drag force acting against an object moving through water, air, or other medium

economy of scale reduction in the cost of producing each item when a larger number of them are produced. The cost of each item falls because the total cost of production is spread across a greater number of items.

engineering use of mathematics and science to design and build structures, machines, devices, systems, and processes

environmental impact effect something has on the natural world

exhaust emissions gases and particles given out by an internal combustion engine

fuel cell device that uses a chemical reaction between a fuel and oxygen to produce electricity. The fuel is usually hydrogen or a substance that contains hydrogen.

hybrid car car with two different types of engine. The most common type of hybrid car is the hybrid electric car, which has a normal internal combustion engine and one or more electric motors.

life cycle all the stages in the lifespan of a plant, animal, or product, from beginning to end

machine tool machine used for changing the shape of a material by using cutting tools

machining manufacturing process that involves changing the shape of a part by using machine tools to drill holes in it or cut material off it

patent authority from a government that allows a manufacturer sole right to make a product or component

prototype one of the first examples of a product to be made, so that it can be tested to make sure it works properly

quality control system for ensuring the high quality of a manufactured product by inspecting it and testing it

raw materials simplest or most basic materials from which a product is made

recycling processing old materials and products to make new materials and products. Recycling saves raw materials and reduces waste.

sensor device that measures a physical quantity such as temperature or pressure and converts it into an electrical signal

simulation realistic images or models of cars in real-life settings to show how a new car might look in the real world. The moving parts of a car or its engine may also be simulated by computer to make sure the parts fit and move as they should before they are manufactured.

stamping manufacturing process in which sheets of metal are pressed to form a different shape. A car's body panels are usually made by stamping.

suspension springs and other parts that link a car's body to its wheels. The suspension system lets the wheels move up and down to follow the shape of the ground while the body glides along more smoothly.

system set of things that work together to do a job. All systems have an input, a process, and an output.

troubleshooting process of solving problems or correcting faults in designs or products

turbine device that uses the energy in a flowing gas or liquid to make a shaft rotate. A turbocharger in a car uses the exhaust gases rushing out of the engine to turn the shaft.

FIND OUT MORE

Books

Car Science, Richard Hammond (Dorling Kindersley, 2011)

Cars and Motorbikes (Sci-Hi: Science and Technology), John Townsend (Raintree, 2012)

Fast Cars (How Machines Work), Ian Graham (Franklin Watts, 2008)

How Cool Stuff Works, Chris Woodford, Luke Collins, Clint Witchalls, Ben Morgan, and James Flint (Dorling Kindersley, 2008)

Websites

www.renault.com/en/innovation/au-coeur-de-la-technique/pages/au-coeur-de-la-technique.aspx

The French car manufacturer, Renault, takes a look inside cars.

www.toyota.co.jp/en/kids/car/index.html

Toyota takes you through the whole car manufacturing process. Another part of their website, **www.toyota.co.jp/en/kids/eco/index.html**, deals with car recycling and hybrid cars.

www.tomorrowsengineers.org

Visit this website to find out how to plan for a career in engineering.

Places to visit

Brooklands Museum, Weybridge, Surrey

www.brooklandsmuseum.com

Brooklands has historic links with British motorsport and aviation. It was the world's first purpose-built motor-racing circuit when it opened in 1907. Some of the original buildings and part of the track survives to the present day.

National Motor Museum, Hampshire

www.beaulieu.co.uk/attractions/national-motor-museum

Britain's National Motor Museum houses more than 250 vehicles at the historic Beaulieu Abbey in the New Forest.

Galleria Ferrari, Maranello, Italy

www.ferrari.com/English/about_ferrari/Ferrari-Museum/Pages/Home-Museo.aspx

Visit Ferrari's museum, the Ferrari factory, and the track where its cars are tested.

Museum of Transport and Technology, Auckland, New Zealand
www.motat.org.nz
New Zealand's biggest transport and technology museum, known as MOTAT, is one of Auckland's top attractions.

In addition to these national museums, many towns and cities maintain smaller transport museums, and individual car manufacturers often have their own museums dealing with the history of their own cars.

Topics for further research

- Car safety: see what you can find out about the safety features that are built into cars and how they work. How does an air bag know when a car is crashing? What material is a seat belt made of, and why? How does an anti-lock braking system (ABS) stop a car more safely?

- The environmental impact of cars: which gases does a car engine give out? Why are some of them harmful? Why was lead added to petrol and why was it later removed from petrol? How do cars and other vehicles affect the air, especially in busy cities? How do catalytic converters reduce harmful engine emissions?

- The future of cars: how do you think car design might change in future? Will we still have petrol-engine cars 10, 20, or 50 years from now? Which new car technology will be the most popular – battery power, fuel cells, or maybe hydrogen fuel? Or will we all have driverless robot cars by then?

- Road-building: who built the first roads – where and when? How did ancient roads compare to roads today? What is a modern road made of? How often do roads have to be rebuilt or resurfaced?

- Oil, from oil-well to fuel station: find out how oil is brought up from underground and processed in a refinery to make petrol and a variety of other fuels and chemicals. Where did the oil come from? What is it? How did it form? Where in the world is it found? When and where were the first oil wells drilled?

INDEX